with the dead has been: Love is come a-gain, like wheat that spring-eth green.

In the grave they laid him, Love whom men had slain, Think-ing that ne-ver

*Descant voices taken from Sopranos.

*If required the basses may sing the tenor line to help pitch their entry in bar 47.

2. Love Divine Is Coming
(Advent)

Words & Music
PETER SKELLERN

*Piano accompaniment optional.

© Copyright 1998 Novello & Company Limited

3. Lullaby

After all the noise and commotion of the visiting shepherds and wise men the Virgin Mary is left alone with her baby

Words and Music by
PETER SKELLERN

*Piano accompaniment optional.

© Pendulum Music Ltd., London W1Y 3FA
Used by permission of International Music Publications Limited.

18

4. Were You There?

The singing should be as crisp as the piano part, bright and staccato.

Words and Music
PETER SKELLERN

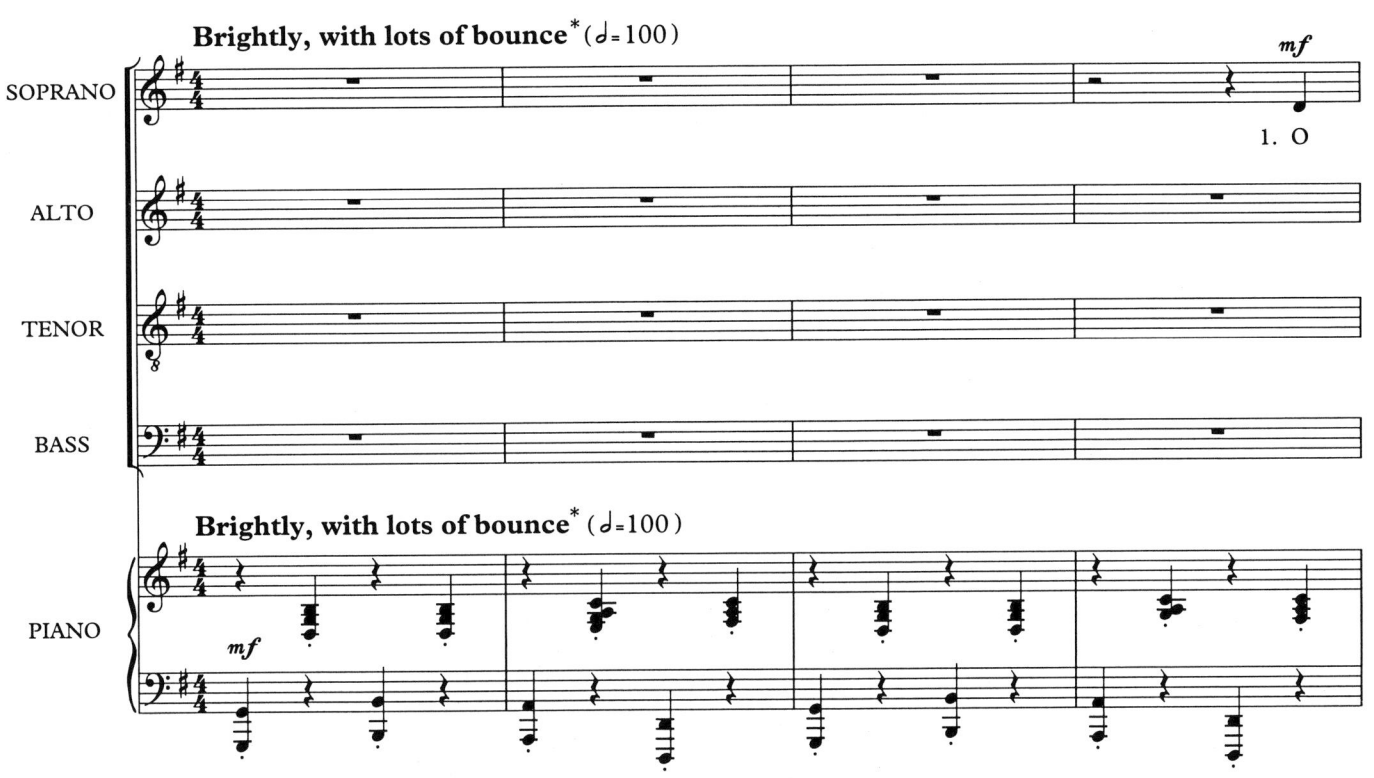

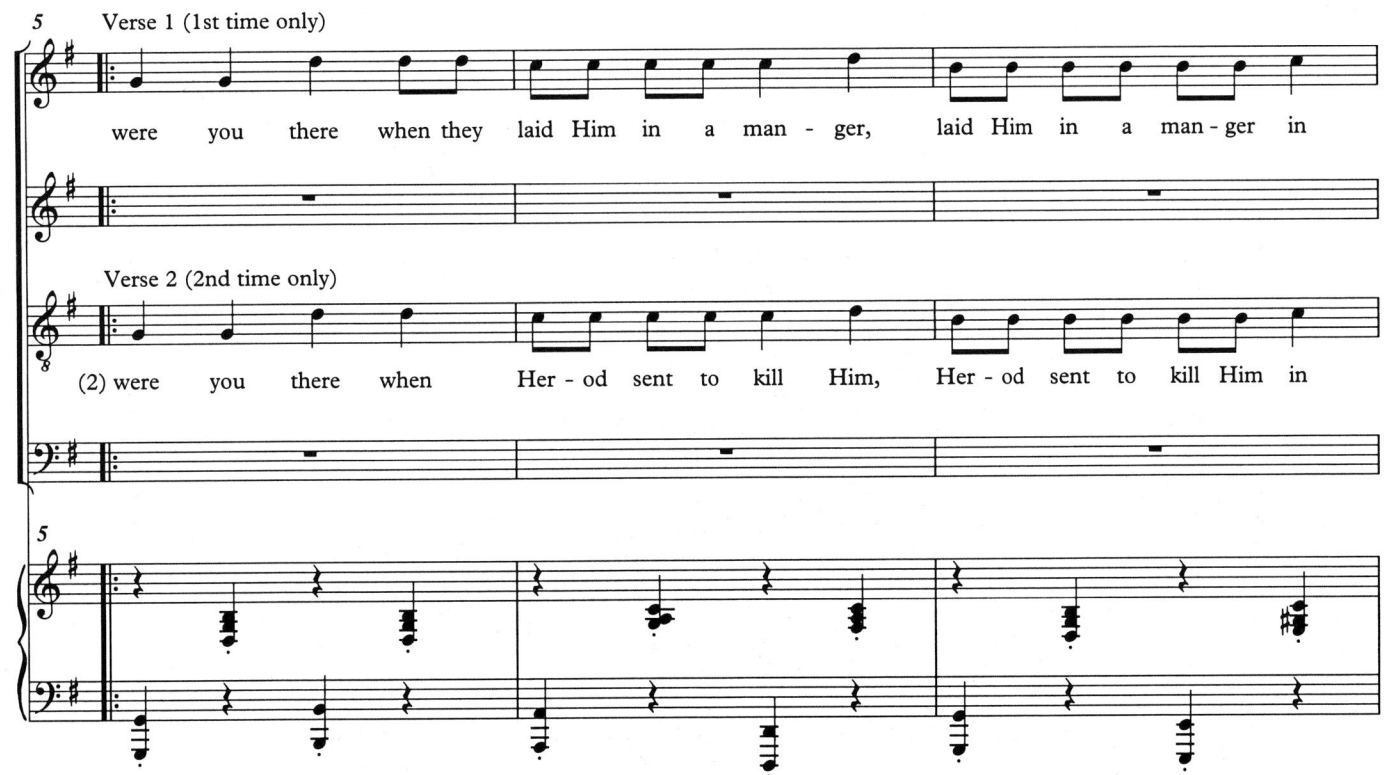

* The tempo should be as swift as the diction will allow, but no faster than the tempo marking.

© Pendulum Music Ltd., London W1Y 3FA
Used by permission of International Music Publications Limited.

5. How Long The Night

*An old man, who in his youth was a shepherd boy,
tells Luke of the night when the world changed*

Words & Music
PETER SKELLERN

*3rd time only **Piano accompaniment optional
© Copyright 1998 Novello & Company Limited

9
1,2
draws us near, for the Son of God, our Sa - v'our, is
glo - r'ous dawn when the Son of God, our Sa - v'our, was born.
heard His name, when the Son of God, our Sa - v'our, came.
draws us near, for the Son of God, our Sa - v'our, is here,
div. p
9
13
3
Long Pauses
mp
p
pp
here, our Sa - v'our is here.
unis.
div.
13

41

6. So Said The Angel

Words and Music
PETER SKELLERN

* Women's voices divided into three equal parts
** These staccatos are crisp, but not 'cold'.
† Piano part optional

© Copyright 1998 Novello & Company Limited

11
mf
free. He said he brought glad ti - dings of com - fort and joy to all,
mf
free. He said he brought glad ti - dings of com - fort and joy to all,
mf
free. He said he brought glad ti - dings of com - fort and joy to all,
mp
Ooo
mp
unis.
Ooo
11

15
said He came to save us all from such sor - row,
said He came to save us all from such sor - row,
said He came to save us all from such sor - row,
p
Ooo
Ooo
div. p
Ooo
Ooo
15
p

19
mp
save me from such sor - row
p
so said the an - gel
Ooo
23
Said the an - gel.
pp
Ooo

29
mf
He has come to raise me, born, he
36
said, to make me strong. He said he brought glad tid - ings
f

45

* Descant voices taken from Soprano

47

48

Published by Novello Publishing Limited, 8/9 Frith Street, LONDON W1V 5TZ
Distributed by Music Sales Limited, Newmarket Road, Bury St Edmunds, Suffolk IP33 3YB
Music setting by Stave Origination
Printed in Great Britain by Caligraving Limited Thetford Norfolk
4/07 (62108)

ISBN 0-85360-894-6

Peter Skellern

SIX SIMPLE CAROLS

for SATB chorus (with optional piano accompaniment)

Novello
Order no. NOV 290698

SIX SIMPLE CAROLS

1. Love Is Come Again
(Easter)

Words
J.M.C. Crum

Old French Tune
arr. PETER SKELLERN

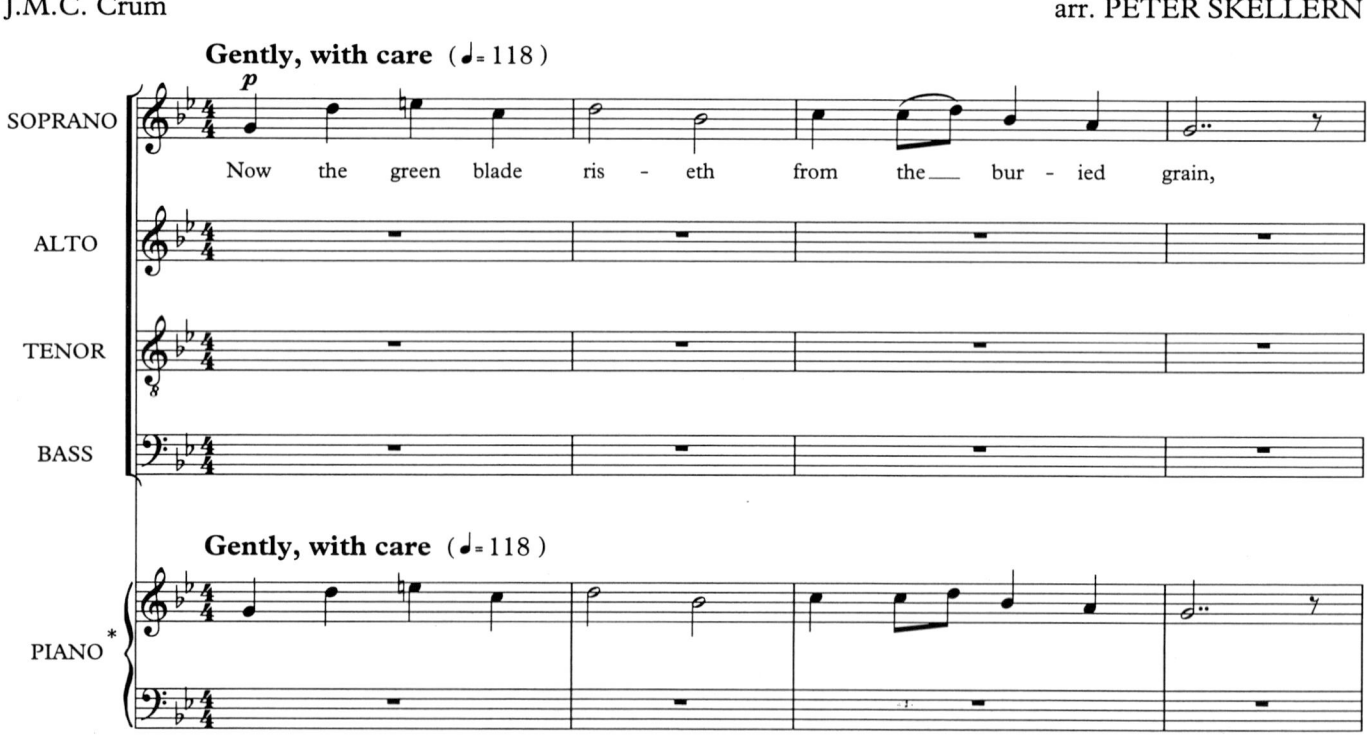

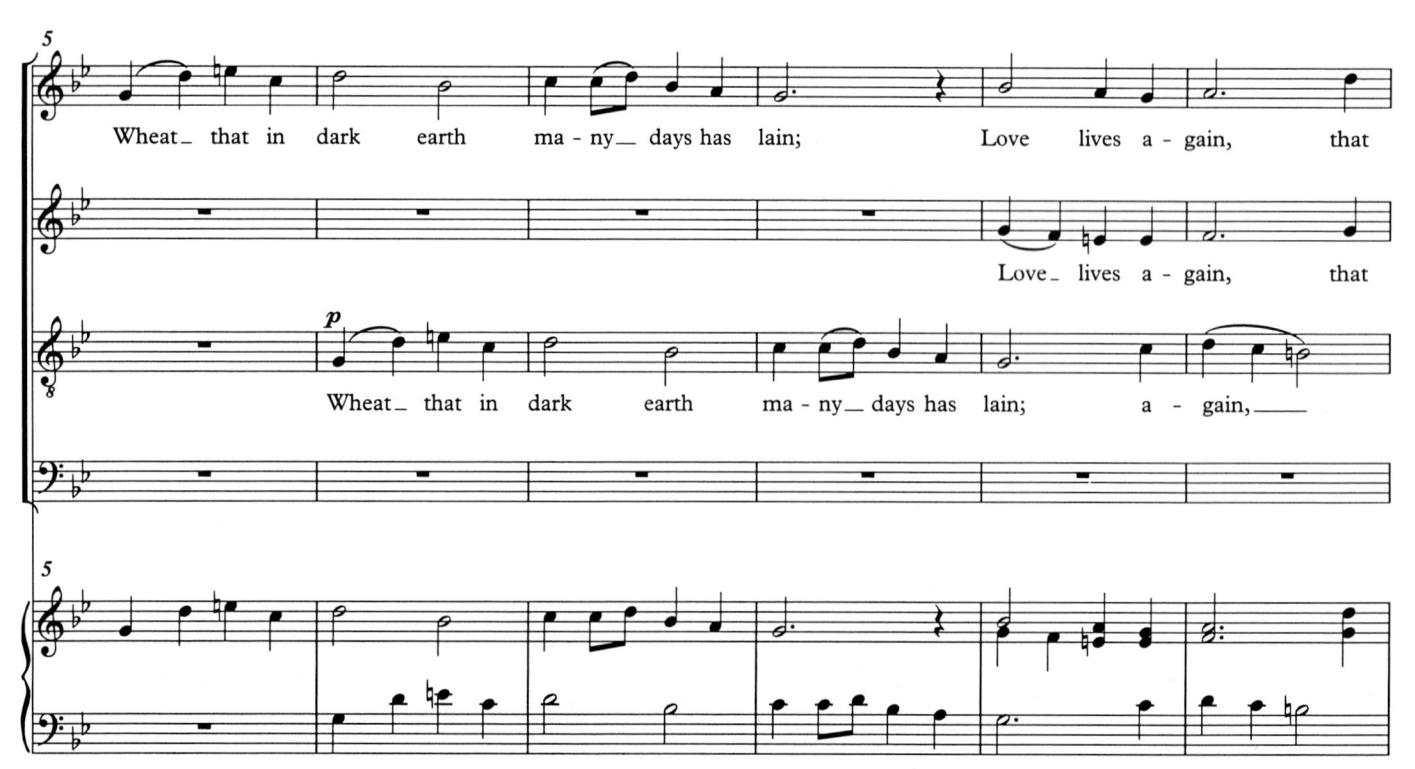

Now the green blade riseth from the buried grain,
Wheat that in dark earth many days has lain; Love lives again, that

*Piano accompaniment optional.

© Copyright 1998 Novello & Company Limited
Words copyright © Oxford University Press 1928. Reproduced by permission.